Saint Germain

Manifestation

Magic

Gordon Corwin II
aka
Lah Rahn Ananda

Saint Germain

Portrait by Marius fine Art

ALL RIGHTS RESERVED
INCLUDING THE RIGHT OF REPRODUCTION
IN WHOLE OR IN PART IN ANY FORM

HIGHLAND LIGHT PUBLISHERS IS
A REGISTERED TRADEMARK WITH THE U. S. PATENT
AND TRADEMARK OFFICE. GORDON W. CORWIN II

Manifestation Magic
First Edition 2023
Highland Light Publishers

All rights reserved. No part of this book may be used or reproduced by any means, graphic, electronic, or mechanical including photocopying, recording, taping, or by any information storage retrieval system.

This Work may be ordered
by visiting Amazon.com or
Barnes and Noble.
or through independent and chain book sellers, online retailers worldwide.

The views expressed in this book are conditioned by the Disclaimer which follows. Certain stock imagery © Dreamstime.com., 123RF.com and Gordon W .Corwin II.

Oceanside, CA. 92056-6237
Copyright © 2023 – Gordon W. Corwin II Lah Rahn Ananda

Volume IV

MANIFESTATION MAGIC

Beyond the Veil

*Spirit Sourced * Human Made*

AI Free

TABLE OF CONTENTS

CELESTIAL PURPLE	INTRO
OVERVIEW	1
INTRODUCTION TO MANIFESTATION	5
EXAMPLES OF MANIFESTATION	7
ALCHEMY	9
POPULAR TALK OF ATLANTIS	11
THE SHOCKING TRUTH	13
CONSCIOUSNESS PERSPECTIVES	15
IGNORING COSMIC BALANCE	17
OBSESSION WITH TECHNOLOGY	19
YOUR LIFE JOURNEY	21
'MY INTENTION' SAINT GERMAIN	27
MYSTERY OF MANIFESTATION	29
SYNCHRONICITY AND SERENDIPITY	33
JETTISONING YOUR EGO	45
WHAT ABOUT FEAR AND DUALITY?	53
'MY ASSURANCE' SAINT GERMAIN	59
SURRENDERING TO THE OUTACOME	61
THE SPARK OF BEING SUPER HUMAN DIAGRAM	67
JUDGMENTS AND HEALING	69
TRANSCENDING INTO UNCONDITIONAL LOVE	71
HIGHER DIMENSIONAL ONENESS DIAGRAM	75
SAINT GERMAIN'S TOOLBOX DIAGRAM	81
BOOKS BY THE AUTHOR	83
THE CLEANSING PROCESS	85
ENTERING THE SPACE OF MANIFESTATION	91
THE PROCESS ELEMENTS	97
IN CONCLUISION	99
ABOUT THE AUTHOR	101
LIGHT OF THE SOUL FOUNDATION (501)(C)(3)	105
HAPPINESS	106

OVERVIEW

True Manifestation has long been a desire of Humans, a yearning to magically possess abilities to somehow blend the Human Condition with mysterious powers to transform and materialize energy into new forms. Earthly cycles through the Ages have historically witnessed the birth, rise, flourish, reign, and fall of Human civilizations, as Atlantis, ... where Manifestation, both aligned and distorted, played a vital evolutionary role for Humanity upon Planet Earth.

Saint Germain "This *current period* of Mankind's upward cycle highlights a revived interest for Intaking and Understanding Spiritual Truths *Beyond the Veil*, along with the concurrent exponential explosion of technological discoveries, *obsessing* the Global focus of Mankind. And the *troubling Truth* for All Humanity is simply that the Manifesting of Mankind's advances in technology grandly outpace a clearly stuck, stagnated, and imbalanced consciousness steeped in Separation, conflict, and *disregard* of the *Consciousness of Oneness need to now prevail, embracing* widespread choices for the Highest Good of ALL.

This work, *Manifestation Magic Beyond the Veil*, focuses upon accelerating Your Loving expansion of a balanced, Enlightened consciousness, individually learning to Manifest in Divine surrender Beyond the Veil, with a quantum leap-forward training to realize and remember your own magnificent Human potential and Divinity living within". St. G.

Blessings to All,
    Lah Rahn Ananda aka
    GORDON CORWIN II

reetings once again, My Beloved Chelas and You of casual interest as well. I come to You now to expand upon the Third-Dimensional secular framework of Manifestation given previously in My book *'The Saint Germain Chronicles Collection'* published in 2016.

To begin, I cordially invite You to join Me in my Etherical crystal cave of Light, brilliantly sparkling for You, an honoured guest in this, My Ascended lair. Although there are many aspects to the energies of Manifestation and Alchemy, today I shall elucidate those aspects that may *seem* to You to be Magical, … while you share this territory of My turf, and intake My vibrations as the Maha Chohan Ascended Master of the Aquarian age.

Allow Me to introduce Manifestation

Behold anew, … for the mass of Earthlings, this is an elevated state of Being involving a fundamental thought process of materializing energy *into different forms* … infinite forms of transformation that may result in new and startling Human realities, not only as congealed matter, but also resulting as energy in inspiring forms new to you.

Some examples of Mysterious Manifestations in Action, *understandable yet not all Humanly achievable, include*:

Synchronicities,
The Moving by thought of congealed Earth matter in Physical form,
Telepathy, Bi-location
Shapeshifting,
Healing,
Reception of channeled Masters' energies,
Transmissions between a Human and Ascended Masters,
Materialization and/or dematerialization of *Human and animal forms*,
Materialization of *energy forms*,
Raising Human body vibrational frequencies above Human visibility,
Transmission of Light energy
Disintegration of negative energy quantums,
Transmitting thought into consciousness of Human individuals and/or masses upon Earth,
Expanding and/or contracting amplitudes of energies (incarnated or shapeless of form),
Teleportation,
Contact with Cosmic civilizations,
… and a multitude of other phenomena, some far *beyond the reach* of your Human understanding and capabilities.

Alchemy

Alchemy is a related phenomenon. For clarity and definition of terms, let Us say that Alchemy is a Magical Process of transforming *matter already in form* into a different materialized form ... a reorganization of molecules, (if you will, Master chuckles, hmmmm).
Sananda demonstrated the transformation of water into wine, as an Alchemical example for Humanity to behold.

And so, We have Alchemy as a subset, if you will, of the Grand Realm of Divine Manifestation.

Suffice it to say for this day, ... that all Humans upon your Planet Earth at this time have the Blessed Divine Opportunity to recall and to re-develop a FOUNDATION FOR DIVINE MANIFESTATION, ... here and now, Folks. Let this work be your guide.

Popular this day is talk of Atlantis.

Know clearly that your FOUNDATION needs to include matters of *both* CONSCIOUSNESS AND TECHNOLOGY similar to *Atlantean Being*.

Upon Earth in this YOUR current Human civilization Period circa 2000 A.D. *Humanity is possessed about advancing its technology with the sad and destructive* EXCLUSION OF CONSCIOUSNESS EVOLVEMENT.

Note as we proceed here, that an ==elevated consciousness will be absolutely required== for you to qualify to Truly Manifest as I have above described.

An elevated consciousness was indeed achieved in Atlantean times. I pray that Humanity at this point will wake up and rise to hurdle this high bar clearly set and Mastered by Atlantean consciousness that also integrated vast technological advances.
At its flourishing height, before the split, the Atlantean collective housed an Enlightened consciousness of Oneness over practicing Separation, laden with rampant greed, material selfishness, debauchery, domination, and darkness.

Shifting the Focus of Human Intelligence toward Higher Consciousness Evolvement.

Especially in this *current civilization cycle, MANKIND IS IN DIRE NEED OF A COURSE CORRECTION!*

A shift of emphasis needs to take place immediately from a predominantly Ego based obsession with Technological Advancement, ... to <u>an energy force</u> that
EQUALS
Mankind's emphasis on <u>evolution and purification of consciousness</u>, both individual and collective!

The shocking TRUTH

<u>To sustain</u> the current pace of Humanity's technological discoveries and advances (circa 1940-2050 A.D.) ... the full Earth consciousness will need to shift from an indulgent base of Ego-separation, fear, greed, domination, weaponization, and war on Earth or in Space, etc., ... <u>to a full consciousness of compassion Unity and Oneness embraced by Love, kindness, and the Highest common good of ALL.</u> Take the best page from the Atlantean play Book!

The needed shift for the current Human consciousness, individual <u>and</u> collective alike, requires engagement in the *INTEGRATION PHASE* of Cosmic evolution, a phase that follows Human *Experimentation.* Let the following diagram give you a framework.

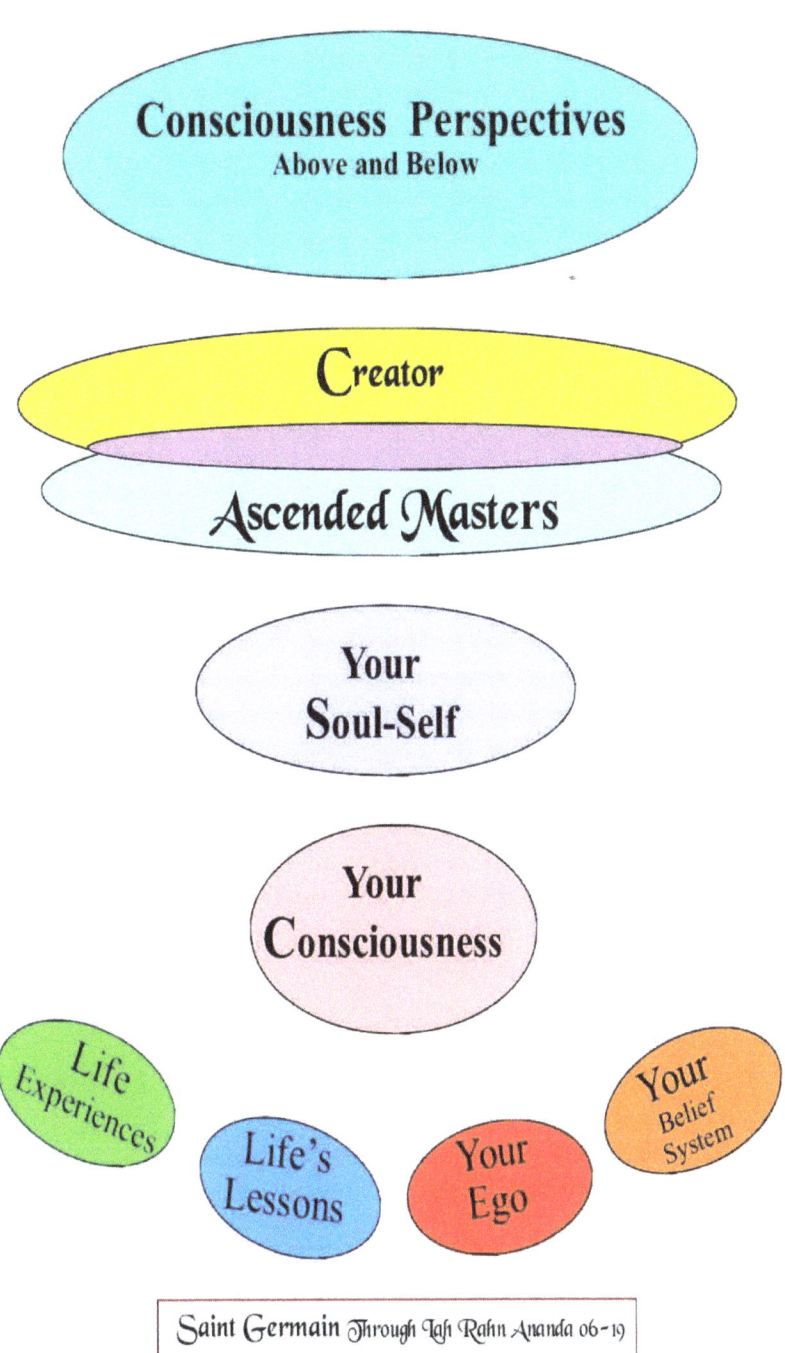

COSMIC reality dictates that an *energy balance* be maintained in place for an Entity to rise into Higher Dimensions and to Sustain that balanced Position, ... an elevated state of wonderous existence enjoyed within *several* other Star Systems in your Galaxy.

This is the Manifestation challenge for your World.
Manifestations for ill-purpose brings in Karma of massive proportions, and this Law shall have its *enduring effect.*

Ignoring this COSMIC balance mandate and Truth will inevitably result in sad Karmic consequences for a brilliant yet defiant Age and Civilization substantially disappearing from the face of Planet Earth, crumbling in the tracks of Atlantis, begging once again for birth of a Human civilization cycle anew.

We Above ask the question:

"Why do Humanity's brightest 3rd Dimensional Minds diligently persist in asking all of the 'right' questions about ATLANTIS for all of the 'wrong' reasons?"
(right and wrong used here, as in your understanding with 3-D vocabulary).

They seek information and secrets of Atlantean technological insights and ... while blindly ignoring questions and *insights about that elevated consciousness that created them!*

Ascended Masters of Spirit sadly observe that the present course of Collective Humanity, *with yourselves included*, continues to indulge in widespread and trendy infatuation and obsession with **raising Earthly technology to greater and greater heights** ... to 'Star Wars' Depictions and beyond, ... albeit with a concurrent collective consciousness steeped in an Earth World of Separation, disharmony, Egomania, and a renegade Global oppressive - authoritarian dark force weaponizing your technology, *upsetting the sacred balance in Cosmic Space.*

See for yourself the deep seeded proclivities of Humans at the highest levels of **Global Governments** historically hungry to harness and weaponize technology with fear-driven Ego motives, ultimately aimed to destroy other Humans, visiting Extra-terrestrials, and affecting the Cosmic balance!

Manifestation of this nature is occurring without a doubt, and as stated here, *it lacks the underpinnings of* **lasting** *and True Divine Manifestation Opportunities which I AM Heartfully intending to now source!*

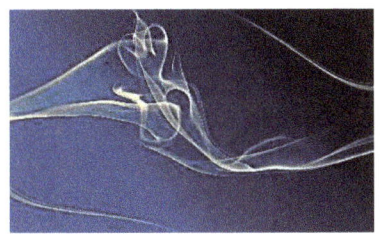

FULLY ADDRESSING the 'Big Picture', … fully comprehending the depth and breadth of such IMPLICATIONS … requires a NEW heightened aligned awareness to contain and to use new technology according to the Consciousness of Oneness and for the Highest Good of All.

Manifestation Magic, Beyond the Veil, is presented here for you as a healing, evolutionary step upward, … to reveal a process of Change … a pathway for you to build a FOUNDATION TO EMBODY CAPABILITIES required to Manifest.

Your important part in this Life journey, as an individual within the collective, … is to Master Manifestation with Oneness, Light, aligned purpose, and Cosmic balance in full effect.

Ascended Spirit Above curiously observes Humanity *moving through and possibly nearing the end* of this particular (approx.) **26,000 year Human civilization cycle.**

Consciousness corruption is the end culprit and reason for collapse.

Your work of consciousness healing is cut out for you, Folks!

Alright! Let the healing begin!

With all of this in your craw, begin to appreciate the gravity of the situation, and to open your Heart and Mind to the beauteous possibilities for a marriage to the Divine Mind, as you now learn to Manifest.

Preparation and Balance

Daring to even approach realizing your Manifestation Magic capabilities without first building a new and solid Foundation upon which to stand, … is pure folly, Ladies and Gentlemen, Boys and Girls!

> **M**y sterling intention here in creating this Dissertation, is to *guide and assist you in finding your way along the high road, ...* to remember, learn, develop, and acquire this **FOUNDATION.** Then and only then will you be qualified to enter the arena of **Manifestation Magic.**

We applaud Planet Earth's technological advancements. They have contributed in some ways to a higher quality and ease of life. Without a doubt, some of Earth's technology is moving in the direction of paralleling *Atlantean* developments reaching back, if you are fascinated with labels, to circa 25,000 B.C. and earlier.

Observe your Mass of Humanity that is blatantly BLIND to the other balancing parts of the evolvement equation. *More and more technology need not be the whole motivation here for Planet Earth.*

As you read along, ask yourself if you would *individually* have had a clue about the missing part of your life's equation? Ponder this question if you will, before reading on.

Yes, your Spiritual IQ is being tested.

☙❧

Mystery of Manifestation

Herein We come together to witness the mystery which surrounds seemingly unexplained phenomena and events, often created by Manifestation and in turn presented unto You by Ourselves as Heavenly gifts into your life stream. Synchronicities discussed below are merely some infinitesimal examples of Manifestation Magic. Read on, Good People!

Along the sequential unfoldment *process of your Earth life*, much of My Divine Magic may be revealed to You, like viewing one of Your Earth cinemas, unfolding an ongoing story upon your video screen.

In the flow of your aware life-stream, You are charged with taking dominion over Your thoughts, emotions, and actions, in the same sense that as St. Germain, I have dominion over the territory of Manifestation from Above.

Follow Me, and I will be *assisting* You in moving toward achievement of your enlightenment about Manifestation in general and specific, ... as well as in gifting you with many magical events in Your life, ... *transpiring with the influence of Source, beyond your reach or grasp.*

At this juncture in your journey, let Me distinguish for you between Divinely dispensed true Blessings of Synchronicity, as a form of Manifestation, and more common occurrences of what *you call Serendipity*. Serendipity, a term often used in Earthly man-made religious circles, emanating from u n e x p l a i n e d , unknown *random events of chance, ... somehow shows up in Your* Earth life. Many such events are nonetheless regarded by Humans as being beneficial, comforting and positive.

Divine Synchronicities

In contrast, however, Divine Blessings of Synchronicity are quite a different matter, as they are *intentionally dispensed* by the Ascended and Angelic realms of Spirit as particular gifts of Love, intended to encourage you of Our lasting presence, ... and to spin and swirl these beneficial and positive energies into your circumstances and evolvement process, especially now as you are beginning to remember more of your Divinity.

We Ascended are empowered to deliver these strokes of Magic into Your daily lives, often times unexpected, delightful, and surprising gifts from the sky.

The arrival of <u>Synchronous Blessings</u> often lifts off the hat from the head of the astonished and bewildered One receiving Our energies. And this is sweet, because such Blessings are at first very foreign to you and cannot be called forth by You, ... unto Yourself or unto others. Above your pay grade, you might say.

These gifts are brought and lain in Grace at the feet of those of You who would be *surrendered and engaged in purifying your evolvement with Trust, Love, and Truth actually <u>living</u> in your very core ... beyond the inquiry and intake steps in your Process. Diagram pp 81.*

Synchronicity embodies the <u>aura of aligned energy</u> called forth by Spirit while evoking the Magic of Manifestation.

<u>Acknowledging Synchronicities</u>

When these magical events light up your daily life-stream, you are wise to pause and take heed, ... to recognize what has just happened, *and to take a moment of time out from your precious and personal Earthly agenda,* to express to the

Creator and Holy Spirit and to the Ascended Masters, your never-ending and unconditional *Gratitude* for Our services, gifts, and Blessings.

   As you will soon observe <u>many integrated elements of a surrendered consciousness are needed to cross the high bar of *Aligned* Manifestation.</u>

   <u>Along this journey, You will be required to give up countless habits of your Ego</u>, stubbornly demanding their illusionary place of high honor in your every-day thoughts, behaviors, actions. and ways of Being.

As you journey forward in this Human lifetime, an urge for Manifestation inevitably raises its head at some point. That is why you are here now with Me, yes?

Perhaps inspired by a desire, need, or even an illusionary crisis, you find yourself at this point, ... now open and ready to intake

the Wisdom you need to effectively shape and develop your consciousness, while learning more about Being <u>fully</u> Human.

Along this particular path of learning while attending the *School of Mother Earth*, We Above can guide you through Manifestation's twists and turns, …provided you grant *your full free-will permission* and follow Our instructions to the letter, *engaging with Love and open Heart!*

With Us standing by in the wings during your process, you shall have Our Love, guidance, and assistance as Ascended Masters, accompanied by Archangels with bells, to assist you in garnering needed energies of Heart, mind, body and Soul.

From the Angelic Kingdom will come Legions of Angels and Archangels, who are ready to embrace you with Love, ushering in ease and grace around your life-walk of Dharma … playing itself out.

Be comforted to know that Our Archangel Michael stands ready at the helm to serve and protect your *best interest* in the Highest Order.

Call to the Angels for support as you remember and learn to Manifest for Divine purpose, once again.

Sobering as it may be, realize that *Aligned Manifestation* requires many of the <u>elements of true enlightenment</u>, *elements needed to be <u>simultaneously</u> focused, congealed into form, and subsequently brought into Being.* So, in a sense, you are really going to Manifest the Art of Manifesting! (Master chuckles heartily haaaaa hmmmm).

I AM highlighting the beauteous *Divine nature of your core Being, surrendered to Oneness, ...* a state of Love which many of you may occupy and <u>can now continue to Be ... in these rapidly changing, challenging times upon</u>

<u>Planet Earth</u> ... a slice of *linear* Earth School time that has a <u>finite period remaining</u> visible through the open window of evolvement opportunity. Are you with me? Re-read this paragraph if need be.

So, ... now, here you are ... seeking to Manifest and about to be stunned by the *credentials required.*

Rest now and ingest these My energies, so Lovingly and precisely lain to words for Humanity by My Blessed and devoted Lah Rahn Ananda, a Beloved Earth Partner of Mine and of the entire Realm for some Earth years now.

You may want to thus pinch thyself, traveling along this roadway. Perhaps you wonder if this Divine Manifestation process is too good to be true? Yes? Seemingly creating something out of nothing? This will be up to you.

And, yes Folks, ... There is a rub!

Actually, there is a high cost. There are certain *ways of inevitably jettisoning*, overboard, replaced by Ego-free aligned Highest, .,. parts of *your Being that require* ... to be thrown ... and a surrendered consciousness with the 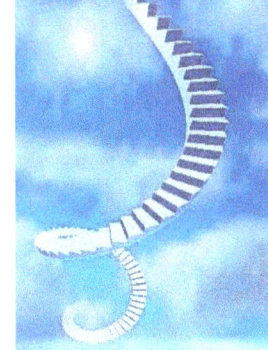 <u>Enlightened Consciousness of Oneness, and with Source, the All of ALL.</u>

   <u>Fulfilling this requirement is requisite</u> for you to receive our Blessings of Manifestation Magic. Have you heard of the Shaman who dies each day to certain parts of himself along his Spiritual journey? Will this be you?

   <u>Much of this consciousness purification work falls upon you, Dear Ones</u>. We fully understand your sometimes *urgent* motivations to engage in Manifestation. We see urgencies that are centered around your beliefs and feelings and requests. We observe requests asking for these 'somethings' to be Blessed, ... the requests are numerous! Often urgent and fearful. <u>My previous discourses</u> speak of the dynamics of 'answered prayers' and how synchronicities are bestowed <u>or</u> denied as unaligned.

Manifestation In Alignment

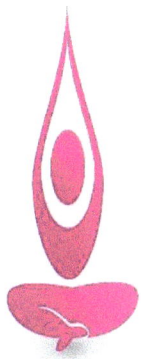

Be truly aware that energy elements of Love, joy, harmony, peace and well-being need be solidly in place surrounding your Aligned Manifestation efforts and Aura.

Exceptions to these requisites, ... deviations from these above elements, excuses, justifications, crying, drama, and whining will fall on deaf ears. You must quality to Manifest in the context We offer. You now know where you stand!

The Human Condition

With higher vibrational energy elements present in your engagement, We also introduce interrelated *Human emotions, feelings, and self-love that play a role.*

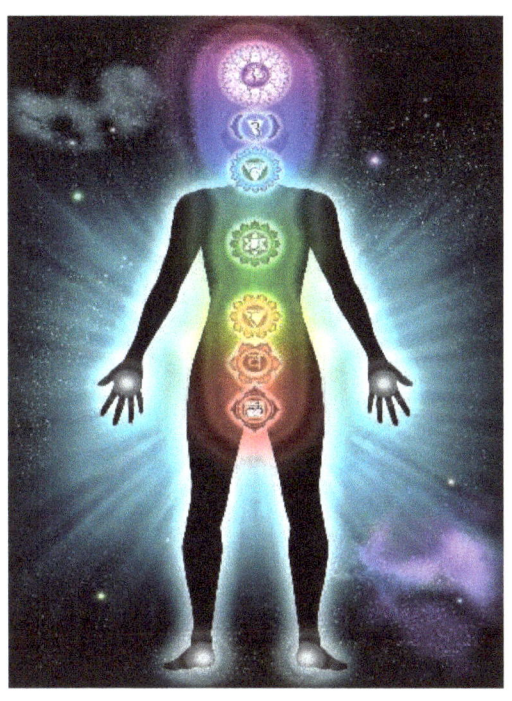

These, coupled with your Human belief system, ... infused with judgments, opinions, self-aggrandizing agendas, and 3rd Dimensional Behaviors, ... all present a plethora of Ego-driven energies which must be *divorced from your Manifestation Magic process and behaviors*, ... ultimately dropped from your day to day, moment by moment life practices.

Another tall order, I acknowledge.

Are you up to the task?

And be aware, <u>you are here</u> in this lifetime in

the *Earth School* to learn and evolve, and to serve. Also, akin to this process, to remember *who you once were* and *who you truly are still.* One who aspires to Manifest in this context will transcend the obstacles I bring to Light here, barriers that would otherwise block your attempted Manifestations from coming into Being.

Alright!

As you will discover in the following pages, there are listed three (3) essential qualifications *at a minimum* for Manifestation Magic. Yet it is not quite that simple, as you hopefully shall soon see. There is a matter of your *Aura adjustment* to radiate the required vibration.

What about your FEAR?

There is a particular common Human emotion I would draw to your attention here. This is fear. Often Fear is an <u>impetus and incentive</u> for your wanting to bring something into Being ... a <u>justification to Manifest</u> ... and to receive *immediate satisfaction of relief! Sound familiar?*

Can you relate to this <u>fear emotion</u>?

Learning about Manifestation without involving Fear, Anger, or Desperation.

Human fear and anger come in all shapes and sizes. They can show up for you as body sensations, thought, or both, and in no particular sequence. It is part of Being Human. Be aware also that Fear and Anger are often connected with your perceptions and reactions to DUALITY.
(Intaking Wisdom about DUALITY may be needed before you can Master this process of fear and anger transmutation).

In brief, <u>Fear and Anger can be processed</u> using focused, rhythmic nasal breathing, daily transcendental meditation, daily aroma therapy, regular exercise, diversion of your thoughts, accepting 'what is', re-choosing your perspective, Gratitude, and having faith in your ability to listen and find a solution to the problem, and more.

Consultation with your Earthly psychologists on Earth may lead you to deal with the source of your fears and anger (not popular coping mechanisms, please). Investigate release therapy.

Let Me interject guidance here to acquire My book entitled: DUALITY *In Perspective*, 2023 Amazon, This work offers a process whereby the effects of Duality are an accepted part of your Life-stream, without man-made negativity or anger. This has bearing upon learning to Manifest. Treat yourself!

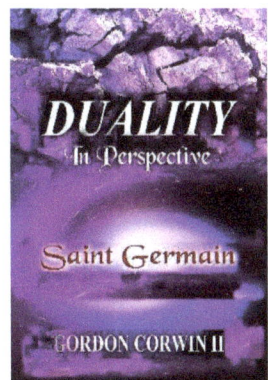

DUALITY In Perspective delivers Masterful guidance with ease and grace, … to transcend *Ego's temptations of becoming resistantly entangled with man-made perceptions about 'good and bad'.*

Many times fear appears *involuntarily*, and then again, you may even *choose fear, possibly as a conditioned reaction of survival or because of pain, or an urge to indulge in an addiction to pain.*

Here is the issue: HOW do you choose to process your fear and to manage it?

> **Remember ... as fear shows up,
> its <u>retention is a choice</u>,
> and suffering can be optional.**

Regardless of fear and anger, Love can <u>simultaneously be chosen</u> to replace them, ... to transcend the fear and anger and their effects, ... *<u>if you have the Faith and courage</u> to Master this process of transmutation.*

Carry on!

Here is the Litmus test!

In the end, clinging to your fear and anger rather than transmuting it with Love and Faith will dictate the quality of your life and *line your pathway.*

Your choice, Your leap of faith, as this is called.

My Assurance

As Saint Germain

Should your Human Earth civilization of current residence *collectively* elect to crumble and fall, and to be once again born anew,

BE ASSURED

You and your SOUL Essence have the power, Lovingly guided by Ascended Beings, to *individually take Dominion over your own Spiritual Destiny, …* to Manifest a continuing path in the Earth School, or to join a Stellar civilization of similar consciousness of Beloved Beings in a destination Star System.

My Dearest Ones,

Enjoy your moments of Being fully Human. I , Saint Germain, will always hold your heart. I will never ever abandon you. I will always Be Here Above, available to Ethereally share My energy with you, in company with the entire Realm of Ascended Masers, at your service.

I will always continue to embrace you with everlasting LOVE, *wherever you may travel.*

I Love YOU.

Saint Germain

Especially for you now, … a *refreshing* morsel of Truth to lift your Spirit. What you are about to next read may, at first blush, seem like your 3-D 'wooo wooo' nonsense, (Master chuckles … hmmm hmmmm), and yet *once you personally experience* this amazing life-changing breakthrough, … this shift of consciousness becomes real for you, resonating in mind, Heart, and body. Read on, My Beloveds. Are you ready?

<u>Surrendering to Yourself.</u>

As you choose surrender without <u>**ATTACHMENT TO THE OUTCOME**</u> … to allow Love to overtake your consciousness, a special feeling and knowing about your Well-being, … a new confidence and detached peace *strangely emerges*. Survival fears are *mystically overturned*, … dissipated into nothingness, … into thin air … far away from your consciousness … *where fear flies of its own accord back into the arms of Heaven that awaits to disintegrate this energy.*

==And the Outcome shall Be as it shall Be.==

<u>*In this enlightened energy field, Manifestation can be born.*</u>

Surrendering is your choice!

So many Humans have told Us this story as an *experience of their new Truth.* I pray it will become yours to also own and tell!

Once you have had this experience, your forever death-grip attachments to outcomes will be released and allow Manifestation Magic to fall into place.

<u>And, yes My Good Friends, there is a codicil to this!</u>

<u>A disregard for what I have just spoken</u> is a common cause for the wheels to come off of the 'wooo wooo' illusion that 'when my fear is gone, I have Spirit's permission to just sit on my ass and do nothing' … because Spirit has handled the circumstance for me!'

Beware of succumbing to this tempting illusion, Folks. *Laziness* is a temptation lurking in the Human Condition. It has trapped many and come back to bite them. You know where, yes! (Master chuckles   Haaaa hmmmm)

You are still Accountable

None of the above metaphysical phenomena withstanding, … you are still accountable to yourself and others to take any *required action or non- action around a circumstance at hand … initiatives needed to resolve, reconcile, complete, and ideally balance the energies that drove you to attempt Manifestation in the first place!*

In other words, allaying your fears does not necessarily get you off of the hook! A re-balanced state, once the fear is dissipated, simply aligns your energies anew to then proceed, dealing with a circumstance in surrendered Divine Love and Alignment. Can you see this?

> **This is a 5 th Dimensional healing process, actually. You are Manifesting a *new purified consciousness, Folks!***

Alright!

Now that We have lain the groundwork, let this evolutionary process be born.
And Blessed.

**Can you appreciate that
<u>The Magical Space of Manifestation</u>
requires considerable Mastery? This is
perhaps the understated question of the era!**

Super-Human traits need be viscerally ingrained, comparable to traits Mastered by 5th Dimensional Human residents upon your plane. Mastering *Manifestation - musts in action* pull you out of the dense miasma of 3rd Dimensional densities. They lift you up with a new and delightful Freedom ... as never before!

And yes, there is more.
Once again, here is another rub!

In certain ways, you will be required to forget much of the customary Third Dimensional behavior that you have been taught, ... habits and behaviors that are *sanctioned by your Society, locally and Worldwide.*

I speak bluntly and plainly of your widespread obsessions to engage in:
JUDGMENTS,
OPINIONS,
FEARS,
DISHARMONY,
SEPARATION,
GREED,
ANGER,
COMBAT,
and more, ...
with total *defiant disregard* for following THE CONSCIOUSNESS OF ONENESS for THE highest Good of ALL.

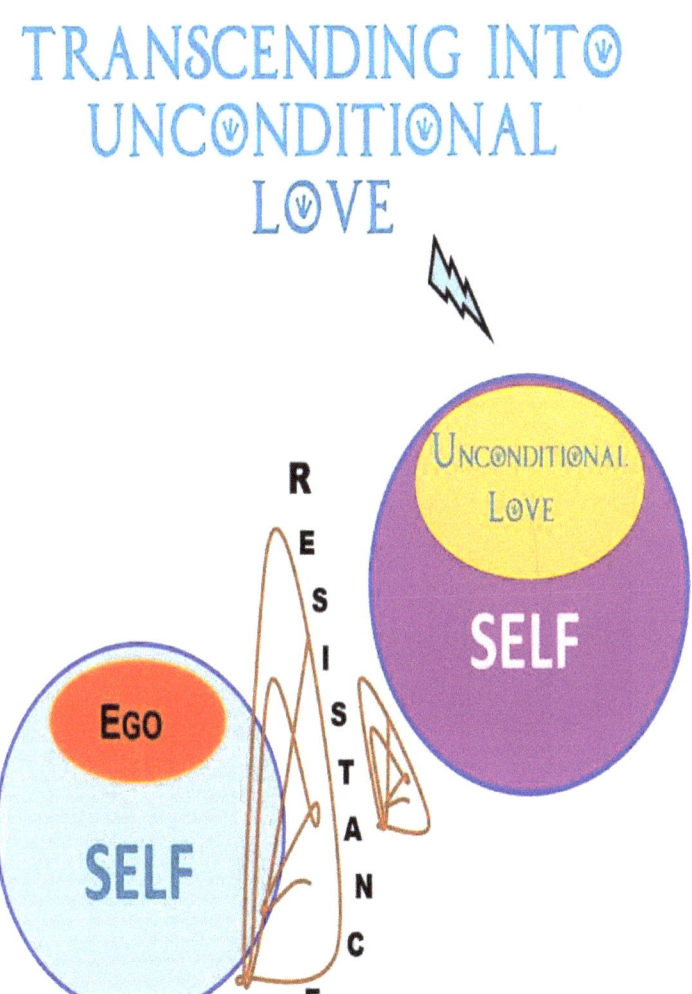

I address here both the <u>individual</u> and <u>collective</u> Human consciousness!

   Rarely do We Above observe Humans in your World behaving with a <u>Win-Win philosophy of Truth</u> in action surrounding all types of their Relationships!
And, this sad state of consciousness, My fine Feathered Friends, … *leads Us to the need for the next part of learning to Manifest.*

You would be well to ==*remember and apply*== *your earlier higher level Atlantean ways of living and Being as We proceed!*

F or most Humans, I Am addressing the urgent need for a <u>complete consciousness overhaul,</u> akin to rebuilding the engine in your car! … and including the carburetor that helps to ignite the *spark of your Divine flame.*

Can you not clearly see that Engagement in the ==Magic of Manifestation== demands your ongoing <u>abandonment of these old Human ways</u> and <u>a shift into the energies of joy, Love, Truth, harmony, abundance, and the Oneness!</u>

   <u>Anything short of this change</u> *will insure your exclusion from the Manifestation you seek. Locked out!* Capisce? This means <u>you doing your Spiritual work!</u> And letting Outcomes Be.

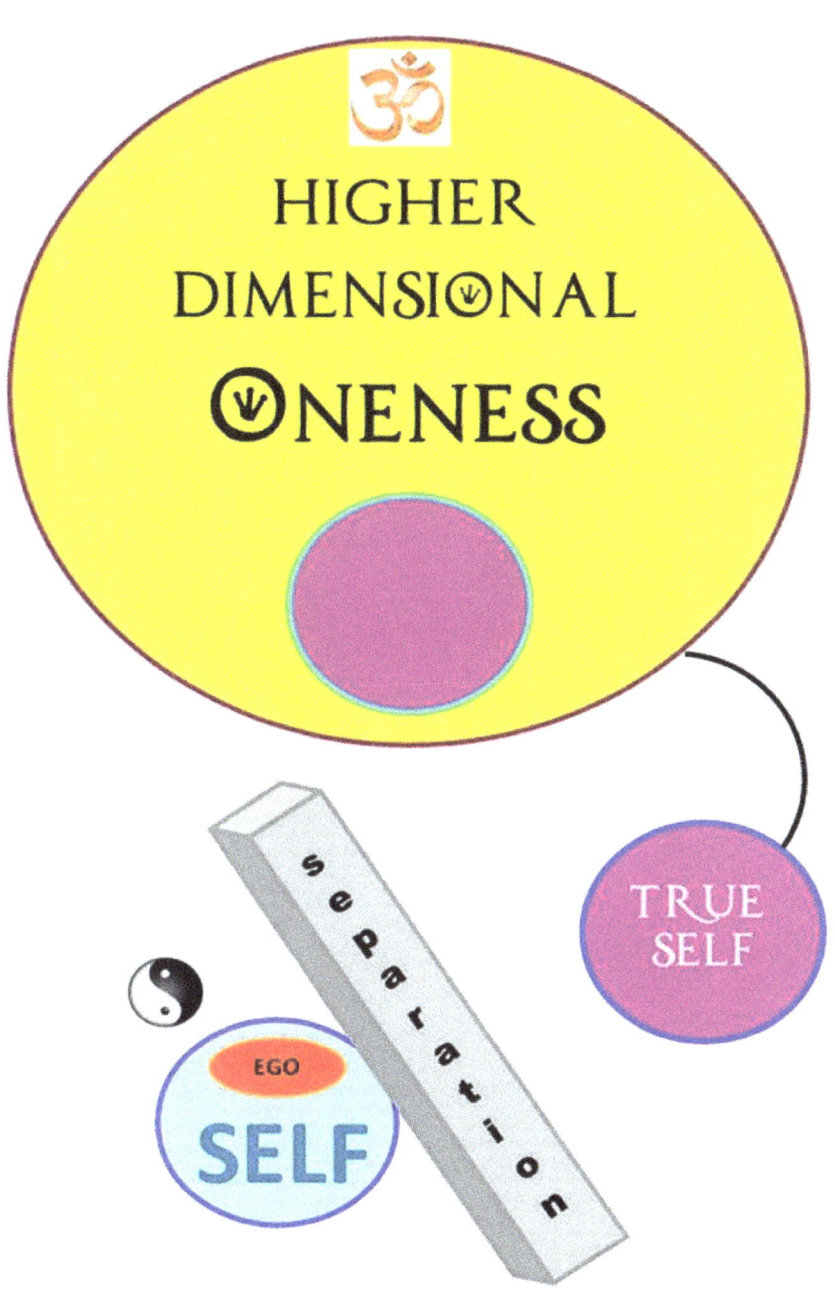

Healing your Judgments into Oneness

- CREATOR
- ONENESS
- COMPASSION
- LOVE
- JUDGMENTS
- YOUR LIFE'S CIRCUMSTANCES

Saint Germain 02-2023

We Above can guide and assist, ... and yet this is your turn to 'stand up, be counted, and fly right', as some Earthlings would say. (Master - Hmmmmm).
The kid gloves are 'off' now, Folks! Here is the litmus test!

And further, ... continuance of the above named obsessions of behavior will reserve your seat in the Third Dimension of the Earth School for this incarnation at a minimum. *Rising Above to Higher Dimensions* entails a ==purified consciousness== and there are no exceptions.

Working your way through these needed changes in consciousness can be eased and accelerated through an engagement in *following the Wisdom I bring forth to Humanity in My latest published book set,*
==*The Saint Germain Toolbox of Wisdom*==.
Applying this Wisdom into your *daily Living* and making *needed changes in your Consciousness will guide you to* unlock *the full Human potential already resting inside of Your Being!*

As Saint Germain, I recommend you now acquire these focused subject Titles which will immensely assist you in tackling Manifestation Magic! Capisce?

The guidance in all of Our books overlaps greatly, though Titles may emphasize certain aspects of Spiritual guidance. They are an essential part of your Spiritual syllabus for evolvement and ultimate Ascension.

ALL of Our books through Lah Rahn Ananda, make up an *interlocking, comprehensive set for your Mastery*, … available to your touch in each moment.

The following set of *Saint Germain Toolbox* books has great bearing on the culmination of your evolvement, and in this context upon Manifestation Magic as a part of this advanced training.

Books by This Author

ରେକ

THE SAINT GERMAIN CHRONICLES COLLECTION
A Journey Into Practical Spirituality

VICTORY FOR THE SOUL
Relationships That Work

RISING ABOVE
A Journey To Higher Dimensions

TRUE COMPASSION
Merging Love Into Oneness

TRUST AND BETRAYAL

DUALITY
In Perspective

GORDON CORWIN II aka LAH RAHN ANANDA   Amazon   www.SaintGermainchronicles.com

The Cleansing Process

This cleansing process I describe will, if you follow My instructions, lead you into the domain of Manifestation Magic that *you so dearly seek as a desire of your highest dreams.*

Alright! As I dispense light unto Your Being wherever you are, as I wave My golden scepter about in the Ethers, gathering the quintessential energy of the moment, I have *Divine license* to then bring down to Earth and unto You a particular Blessing for some particular circumstance. I know you will be grateful!

As You become a more experienced Light Worker and surrendered Devotee of Spirit, You will begin to take note of and utilize My expansive services, ... intaking My energies of Partnership with *consciously expressed gratitude*, which We note well. A wise behavior for your benefit!

<u>You have perhaps heard tell of My Alchemical powers to Manifest</u> by entering into the body of a Human, a raven, an owl, or hawk, for example, and then to fly and sit before you in this form, allowing You to gaze upon Spirit, in that way. In this case, to gaze upon yours truly, Ascended Master Saint Germain, temporarily embodied to further empower You by a physical presence. Humans long to see Me preferably embodied as Human, and also in animal form.

<u>Shape shifting</u> may all seem to you a bit far-fetched, and yet I encourage you to seek out and speak with a select few of My *authentic* Spiritual Channeling Instruments, who have for years *personally experienced* that of which I now speak. Lah Rahn, if you choose. There are others.

A Reminder about Outcomes

Outcomes of Manifestations combine the energies of <u>***all three aspects of the Process***</u> *I shall give to you below.* <mark>Absent any of the three elements</mark> of which I speak, your Manifestation request will receive no endorsement from the Ascended Realm Above. It is the Law.

And yes, some attempts may fall through the cracks and possibly be nonetheless <u>**CONSTRUCTED on your own through Ego-driven Free-will**</u>, in separation, in convoluted form(s), … and out of Alignment, and without Our endorsement. *Needless to say, such attempts / constructions <u>inevitably collapse, disintegrating and dematerializing into nothingness</u>, … in short order! Sad but true.*

Alright!

Now, … and only now … are We ready and prepared to engage in the Manifestation Process. Let all of the foregoing condition You for the Big moment, … to stand upon the *fundamental building blocks of THE FOUNDATION FOR MANIFESTING in your own Earth life.*

Entering the Space of Manifestation

pen your Heart to become fully aware of yourself ... as a small part of a great Universe. ... with your full Being suspended ... peacefully drifting into an open space of serene silence ... within and without ... where no thing takes the place of every thing. You are effortlessly joining and communing with Great Spirit, drifting endlessly into a vast space of Cosmic Oneness. A golden white Light asks to encase your magnetizing energy field ... your Aura is being tuned to a higher frequency.

You will sense this journey as your Being chooses, ... thorough sensations of Light, feelings, visions, and perhaps through sounds.

By now, you are acutely aware that all parts of that *Manifestation in progress* are softly falling in their rightful places ... ready to be brought to Spirit as an aligned request from the Heart chakra, ... acquiring the intensifying golden Light of Love ... building itself to surround ... all around.

A *clear statement of the Manifestation request* can now be refreshed and anchored in place, ... however that may Be, ... verbal, written, or through thought. Gently and peacefully, this request becomes surrounded with Light energy, swirling through your consciousness in tune with Spirit as the *aligned* request transforms, becoming ...

melted, melded, and molded into form.

A *sensing* of the Manifestation may fill your Third eye and/or your entire Being. The impulse is sensed through a highly vibrating intuition mechanism and ability within you, ... a surrendered knowing that this is beyond your field of influence at this point, ... that this is in the hands of Great Spirit, ... a knowing that what shall Be shall Be, ... a willingness to be complete, ... a feeling of Peace.

Occasionally, you may witness Spirit entering, sweeping into the field of other Ones around you, ... those engaged in this circumstance as <u>*surrendered*</u> *ancillary vessels*, albeit from a different level of engagement than yourself.

You may notice a change in their *eyes*, or a general change in their appearance to you, during this Manifestation in progress.

Expressions of these eyes, voices, mannerisms, and Auras are very indicative and rewarding.

At this point, your automatic response of Gratefulness, *a trait of Higher Dimensional consciousnesses*, will surface from within, … and when expressed, your state of Heartful gratefulness becomes known to Great Spirit in that millisecond, … *sparking a return* of Human Energy back to the Realm of Spirit Ascended, … from whence the Manifestation energy originally came. The *Circle of Manifestation Magic* energy is now complete.

With Loving surrender and diligent practice, these Beloved experiences may in time become a repetitive, delightful part of your Human Life-stream, embedded deeply in your Being and Transmuted unto the very Divined core of your Soul essence.

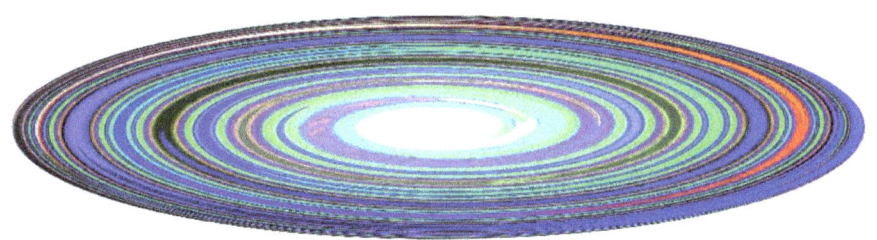

THE PROCESS ELEMENTS

As you vibrate in the forgoing surrendered space you are Heartfully aware that the *Manifestation process involves the harmonious, heart sourced, aligned, and simultaneous interaction between three fundamental elements:*

First, Surrender; the Manifesting aspirant's ability to *surrender* to the Will of Spirit, faith in something possibly unknown; to be crystal clear about the *aligned intention*; to hold no *Ego-sourced attachments* to any outcome whatsoever; detach from *any trace of fear* in this process; and align for the *positive purpose* of holding *the result* in Light and goodness.

Second, Agreement; that there be an *Aligned agreement* between the Earthly Free-wills involved, about the object, means and methods of the Manifestation for Divine purpose.

And Thirdly, Confluence; that a particular request for Manifestation be unconditionally aligned with Laws of the Land, Divine Law, Universal Law and the balancing COSMIC energies of ALL that IS.

Such qualifying Manifestation requests will have Our endorsement and Blessing.

In Conclusion

I AM ethereally delighted and pleased to transmit this advanced work, Manifestation Magic, Beyond the Veil, … unto you, especially at this critical juncture and crossroads for the future of this current Human Civilization.

An enlightened Human Civilization, abundant with Joy, Love, Truth, and Oneness in parallel with advanced Technological Blessings for All in Oneness, … are integral to your Birthrights.

Now, You as an individual, are called to input into your collective the highest vibration of the enlightened Being that you truly are. In the Process, … En - joy every moment of your Human Live-stream, Dear Ones, … joy is also your birthright to claim now and to live.

I urge you to take MY words to heart Dear Friends, as I speak the Truth. I AM forever in your service, delightfully showering Divine and Magical Blessings of Synchronicity to those worthy Ones of You in My care.

Let Me know of your progress, Beloved Ones.
In Light I AM

Saint Germain

Through Lah Rahn Ananda

07 - 14 / 09 - 2023

About the Author

Gordon Corwin II, also known as Lah Rahn Ananda, translated literally as 'God Light Messenger', is a native Californian, educated at UC Berkeley, followed by service as a Commissioned US Naval Officer, and by extensive careers in the computer and real estate industries.

In 1995, Gordon clearly heard Lord Saint Germain's resounding and mysterious voice from Above, recruiting him to immediately engage with Ascended Spirit and follow his Soul's calling to reactivate his considerable past life Atlantean DNA channeling abilities, and to begin walking his Dharma to serve Humanity!

As an appointed Masters' Representative, Lah Rahn then began delivering Ascended energies through channeling of the Masters' words and visual media, which would now become his changed and conscious life path. In 1998 he founded The Light of the Soul Foundation, a qualified non-profit entity for advanced Spiritual education and Human philanthropy.

Following years of ego-cleansing by the Masters, Lah Rahn Ji has, for 25 years now, delivered clear and engaging channelings of public and private Spiritual events along with potent and enlightening mentoring of Chelas in The Light of the Soul Vortex in Southern California.

In 2007 he was highly honored to be chosen by Lord Saint Germain to be the Ascended Masters' instrument and Partner to begin, and later complete, this precise and accurate channeling to Earth of 𝔗𝔥𝔢 𝔖𝔞𝔦𝔫𝔱 𝔊𝔢𝔯𝔪𝔞𝔦𝔫 𝔊𝔥𝔯𝔬𝔫𝔦𝔠𝔩𝔢𝔰 ℭ𝔬𝔩𝔩𝔢𝔠𝔱𝔦𝔬𝔫, *A Journey Into Practical Spirituality 2008-2014*. In 2020 Lah Rahn again partnered with Saint Germain to write Victory for The Soul, *Relationships that Work, pub 2022, and* RISING ABOVE, *A Journey Into Higher Dimensions, pub 2022, Amazon, Gordon Corwin II,* among other unpublished channelings along with those from Quan Yin and El Morya.

Lah Rahn aka Gordon Corwin currently lives in Oceanside, California and is available for private channelings and group events, as well as public speaking engagements.

Contact:
GordonCorwin24@gmail.com
Lah@SaintGermainChronicles.com

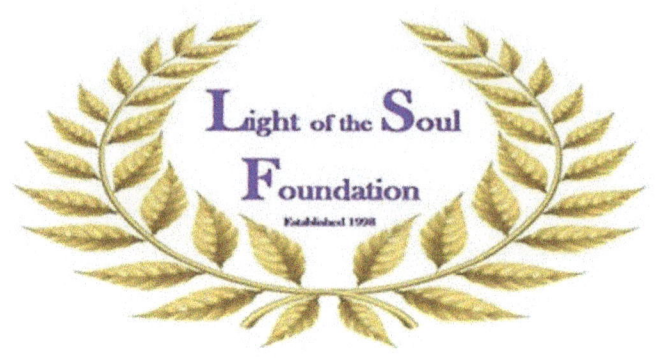

The Light of the Soul Foundation is a Charitable non-profit 501 (c) (3) Philanthropic Organization founded in 1998 by Gordon Corwin, Trustee.

This non-denominational Foundation is dedicated to

The Spiritual Enlightenment of Humanity.

LOSF continues to be harmoniously bonded with

Highland Light Publishers,

sharing this Spiritual mission that includes writing, publishing and distributing Masters' books in addition to delivering live events with wisdom from The Ascended Masters Above.

"Bringing the Light of Spirit into the _every-day lives_
and _consciousness_ of the masses
in an increasingly troubled earthly world
… is the practical gift We lovingly offer".

As you now may observe, the collective behavior of Humanity present dark and pervasive behaviors that prevail without change. Your kind philanthropy, donations, and bequests provide the financial means enabling Us to continue serving and delivering
Enlightenment from Above,
expanding Our outreach of Light.

Your donations are transformed into the highest vibrations to all Ones aspiring to reach and live their full Dharma's potential of heightened awareness, Love, Compassion and Soul evolution … which awaits Humanity.

Light of the Soul Foundation

Charitable Non-profit 501 (c) (3)

Public Events and Spiritual Counseling

 **EIN: 91-1945098**

For Your Gifts, Donations, or Bequest Confirmations,
By Check, Credit Card or Bank Wire.

We are deeply grateful to Donors, Contributors and Philanthropists for your fine and generous *Gifts of Grace to uplift The Human Consciousness.*

You are an
immensely essential resource that ongoingly empowers
Our continuing Outreach.

For two decades, We have delivered gifts of
Soul Enlightenment and Practical Spirituality via
recently published channeled works, along with public events
and Spiritual readings … with your generous support!

Many Thanks and Blessings. *You All* are
Most Appreciated!

Gratefully yours, Gordon Corwin / Lah Rahn

Please Contact: Trustee, Gordon Corwin,
Oceanside, CA 92056

Gordoncorwin24@gmail.com   or
Lah@SaintGermainChronicles.com

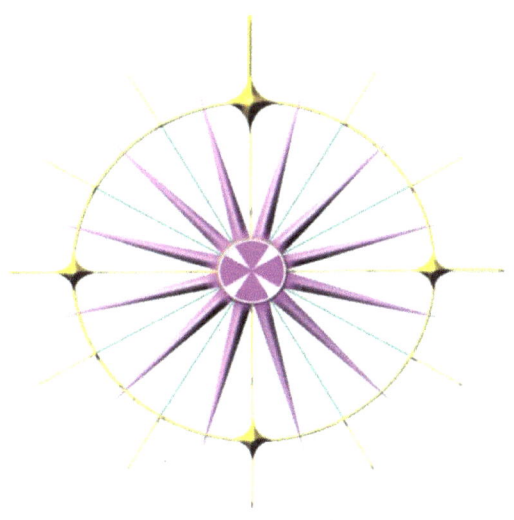

Light of the Soul Foundation

(501)(c)(3)

EIN: 91-1945098

COLORS OF HAPPINESS

An Elevated State of Being

Behold this magnificent euphoric feeling of Peace and Well-being, a Higher Dimensional state of Joy, Love , and Freedom that flows into and rests within your consciousness, ... mind, body, and Soul .... a vibration native to Human DNA, ... with *Free-will t*o choose Love and to Be Loved in ONENESS of the All, ... while *escalating above* conflicting and negative Earthly influences.

Short of such surrendered ways of Being ... while otherwise basking in the status quo harbored by a World of ego–dominated separation ... then comes that all familiar fast-track journey along the slippery slope of hope without action, endlessly searching in vain.

Harken to open those doorways that shall appear in your life-stream ... opportunities to cross thresholds offering delightful respites of Happiness along your journey, be they flashes or long lived. May an open Heart, Self-Love, purified Self-talk, supportive relationships, and Divine embrace pave your path with Light, My Dearest Ones.

Blessings

Saint Germain

Saint Germain

Through
Lah Rahn Ananda
02-15-2024

Blessings
Saint Germain

Through

Lah Rahn Ananda

DISCLAIMER

The information contained within this Book is strictly for educational purposes. This Book and the Book's elements are provided to readers committed to Spiritual education, self-discovery, self-actualization, and transformation to align individual belief systems with a common source, Our Creator and Spirit, as the guiding light to enter doorways of change, new possibilities, growth, and manifestations within reach of an extraordinary and self-examined Human lifetime. Readers are encouraged to choose, of their own free- will and volition, to accept, to follow, or to reject the guidance, ideas, philosophies, stated truths, and techniques presented herein. If you wish to apply ideas and guidance contained herein, you are taking full responsibility for your actions. This Book contains information and general advice that is intended to help the readers to be better informed about physical, mental, emotional, and Spiritual well-being. Always consult your doctor for your individual needs. This Book is not intended to be a substitute for the medical advice of a licensed physician. The reader should consult with their doctor in any matters relating to his/her health. This Book contains information and general advice about business pursuits. This book is not intended to be a substitute for financial or legal advice. Reader is advised to consult your licensed financial or legal professional for such matters. In no event does the author or the publisher make guarantees, express or implied, as to results or consequences arising out of or related to the reader's use or inability to use the book's contents. Both the author and Highland Light Publishers (the publisher) do not assume and hereby disclaim any liability to any party for any loss, direct, indirect, or consequential damages, accidental, unintentional, or unforeseen, pain, suffering, emotional distress, or disruption resulting from the reader's negligence, actions or non-actions, accident, or any other cause.

Copyright 1998 – 2023. All rights reserved by Highland Light Publishers and Gordon W. Corwin II. Reproduction in any form, including foreign translations, radio broadcasts, all publications or storage, electronic or otherwise, may only be done with the express written permission of Highland Light Publishers or Gordon W. Corwin II; such permission will not be unreasonably withheld.

Contact Lah Rahn: Lah@saintgermainchronicles.com

Gordoncorwin24@gmail.com

www.ingramcontent.com/pod-product-compliance
Lightning Source LLC
Chambersburg PA
CBHW050729010526
44107CB00009B/792